101 FLIRTY WRITING PROMPTS TO SEDUCE YOUR MUSE

a gift from

M. JANE COLETTE

For that person at the back of every workshop I deliver, who flushes and blushes and giggles and thinks they can't do it. Yes, you can.

Here's to liberating your inner writer.

Remember to invite me to your book launch party.

GENRES were made to be BROKEN

Cover Art: iStock Photo
Cover Design: M. Jane Colette

First Printing July 2019
GENRES were made to be BROKEN
121, 104-1240 Kensington Rd NW
Calgary, Alberta T2N3P7 Canada

Copyright © 2019 M. Jane Colette
M. Jane Colette asserts the moral right to be identified as the author of this work.

All rights reserved. No part of this book may be reproduced in any form or by any electronic or mechanical means, including information storage and retrieval systems, without written permission from the author, except for the use of brief quotations in a book review.

ISBN: 978-1-989297-08-7 (trade paperback)
ISBN: 978-1-989297-07-0 (ebook)

mjanecolette.com

INTRODUCTION

The What, Who, Why, When, Where and How of Writing Prompts

Writing prompts get you writing when you don't know what to write about. They kill procrastination, silence your inner censor, and teach you how to write in fifteen minute increments. Here's the biggest writing secret of all time: epic novels get written in fifteen minute increments. Don't know how to start? Writing prompts are one of the tools that make this possible.

WHAT

Piano. Feather. River.

That's all you get, those three little words. Now grab a pen and some paper—or flip open your laptop—and start writing. Write for five, ten, fifteen minutes, or write until you're finished. The only rule is—your piece must include all three words. Ready? Go.

No one was surprised when the couch tipped over.

That's the first sentence of your scene. Go. Don't overthink

—just write. Write until the scene feels complete, and you—or your characters—need a cigarette. Yeees... just... like... that.

Setting: hotel room. Your lover is lounging on the bed. You come in through the door. You haven't seen each other in an eternity. The first thing you notice is the carpet... and then... what happens? Write for five minutes.

Hmmm, let's make that one more complicated—you can't use any verbs. Sure, that's possible. Go. Challenge yourself.

Pull a Tarot card. Oooh, the Mother of Wands: creative, vibrant, devoted, fierce, and loyal. She's the character you're writing about in this scene. Go.

Get the idea? A writing prompt can be *anything* that gets you writing. Working with prompts has been a key part of my writing practice ever since I wrote the entire first draft of my second novel, over the course of about sixty days, in response to daily writing prompts. Now, I use writing prompts to keep my writing muscles honed when I'm between novels. Also, to entertain readers at festivals and book signings. *Give me three little words. I'll write you a story that will make your toes curls. I only need five minutes. Time me. Done!*

I use writing prompts in all the workshops I facilitate, even the ones on plotting and organization. And I still use them to work through novels—to get to know characters, to work through the Dark Moment and other convoluted plot points, or to keep myself moving through the Saggy Middle. As every writing teacher worth listening to, from Julia Cameron and Natalie Goldberg on, says over and over again: the secret to writing is writing.

Writing prompts get you writing.

WHO

Everyone can benefit from working with writing prompts. Yes, I mean you. And her and him, and them, and that hyper-prolific guy over there? Him too. I recommend working with writing prompts for writers at all levels of the game, from beginners through to best-selling, mega-productive superstars.

WHY

There are three very simple reasons why I love writing prompts so.

1. Writing prompts are an excellent way of developing a process-focused writing practice that eliminates the dreaded "what shall I write about today" paralysis. The "what" doesn't matter. All that matters is that you write. So. Give me three little words and five minutes, and I'll give you a short dirty story. Done.

2. Writing prompts take you out of your comfort zone and allow you to surprise yourself. Maybe, left to your own devices, you would never start a scene with "The floor was cold and sticky, but…" or "It turned out he did know a thing or two about knots." But that's your writing prompt for the day, and so you do.

Surprising yourself makes for good writing. We all tend to get into our ruts, right? Me, for example, I never describe anything. So giving me a writing prompt such as "Write a scene that takes place under a pendant lamp" forces me to think about setting. Lights, shadows. Furniture. If the pendant lamp is hanging–for that, I think, is what a pendant lamp is–over what is it hanging? A table? An armchair? A table, in a shadowed corner, surrounded by three chairs? Thinking about setting enhances my plot, character development, *everything*. Suddenly, I see three chairs around a table under a pendant lamp, three chairs for four co-parents —which one of them is going to end up chair-less, standing apart from the group? Oh, yes, thank you, writing prompt, family drama, here we go!

3. Finally, writing prompts are an effective and easy way of subverting your inner censor and getting out of your own way. As I keep on harping when I facilitate writing workshops, this thing we call inspiration–it's one part discipline and three parts *not* self-censorship. When you work with a writing prompt, you're not choosing what to write about. (You totally are, but that's the game you're playing with your censor–you're pretending you're just doing what you're told. Not rocking any boats, not pushing any boundaries. Sshh, censor, nothing for you to fret about here.) And, so, because you're not making that initial call, your censor isn't quite sure how to go about stopping you. You're just following instructions. Someone else's instructions. You're being a good little girl. Yes, you are.

Ha. You're so not. Look at all that unbridled, uncensored stuff you're putting down on the page. How did that happen?

Writing prompt, that's how.

WHERE

Where should you write with the aid of your writing prompt?

Anywhere.

Kitchen table, bed, living room floor. Local cafe, park bench, airport waiting lounge. Dentist's waiting room (you need a distraction, right?). Doctor's waiting room (why do these people even bother making appointments if they're going to keep you waiting for two hours?). Hotel rooms and lobbies.

Anywhere.

Everywhere.

When I read advice about how a writer needs a room of her own or how you need a dedicated space... *please*. I live in 1000 square feet with four other people and a stinky dog. I work. I travel.

Professionals learn how to write anywhere.

Not to say that a writing studio or a room of one's own isn't a lover-ly thing to covet. If you're lucky enough to have it, use it and cherish it. But if you don't?

Write anywhere.

Which brings us to...

WHEN

The best time to work with writing prompts is... anytime.

If you're building a new habit, yes, it is helpful to write at the same time each day. I write almost every morning, more or less as soon as I wake up, not because I'm a morning person—sunrises are overrated and alarm clocks are evil—but because that's still the time of day least likely to get derailed for me. If I write first thing in the morning, then, even if everything else that day goes wrong, I'll have written, and no one can take that away from me. And I've been writing in the mornings for such a long time that I don't even think about it. I get up. Pee. Make coffee. Drink water while I wait for the coffee to be ready for my love.

Write.

Except on the days when I need to be somewhere at 6 a.m. I'm not quite that hardcore.

My friend Alyssa writes on most lunch hours at her day job, and a very prolific writer I know gets a lot of his writing done while *not* watching his kids' soccer practices. (I also write while *not* watching my daughter's martial arts classes in the evenings. It doesn't make me a bad mother—screw you, you judgemental helicopter parenting mama giving me the stink eye, you know what five hours a week X 52 weeks X the seven years she's been taking martial arts adds up to? Three million six hundred and forty thousand words, that's what.)

> **PROCRASTINATOR TIP:** When I'm working out something, or trying to reinforce a social media fast, I write a writing-prompt type exercise every time I feel the need to reach for my phone and look at Twitter.

One of my friends wrote her first novel, using writing prompts, when she was working on quitting smoking. She wrote 300 or so words every time she wanted to reach for a cigarette. Three hundred words a day over a year adds up to a 100,000-word novel. Not bad, right?

So. Anytime.

If you can write at the same time each day, especially when building the habit, do it. If you can't, grab that five or 15 minutes whenever you can.

HOW

Using writing prompts involves three very simple steps:

Step 1: Arrange to be fed a writing prompt every day.

From where, from whom? There are thousands, probably millions, of writing prompt sources on the Internet and in your library. Here are 101 flirty writing prompts, based on some of the prompts I use in my writing workshops, to get you started. I also post, depending on what I'm teaching, daily or weekly prompts on my blog and Instagram.

But wait! There's more! Barbara Abercrombie has two terrific books of daily writing prompts, *Kicking In The Wall: A Year of Writing Exercises, Prompts, and Quotes to Help You Break Through Your Blocks and Reach Your Writing Goals* and *A Year of Writing Dangerously: 365 Days of Inspiration & Encouragement*, both of which I've used in my writing practice.

You can also use Tarot cards—I'm currently revising a WIP that I wrote over 78 days using a daily Tarot card as my writing prompt/start. Or, you can follow #writingprompt on Twitter or Instagram. Your choices are, truly, limitless.

PROCRASTINATOR TIP: Get yourself a writing/accountability buddy and commit to exchanging writing prompts at 6 am or 6 pm or midnight every day. I've done this before too, and it's a terrific technique, and not just because it builds peer accountability into the exercise.

Step 2: Write.

Really, that's it, but you can give yourself a few extra rules. If you're a beginning writer, I suggest setting a timer for five minutes the first day, seven minutes the next, and working your way up to a 15+ minute writing session. As an intermediate writer, you should be writing to a natural stop, so that each of your little writing prompt pieces is indeed a scene—with a beginning, a middle, and a natural end. If you're an advanced writer, you should be *edging*—writing until that piece is done, and you can't wait to start on the next one... but you don't. Not yet. (For more about edging, visit *mjanecolette.com/secrets*.)

Step 3: Repeat the next day and the day after.

The organizational and habit gurus say it takes 21-40 days to form a habit. I think they make most of their numbers up. Sometimes we form habits in three days and sometimes we consistently fail to form (or break) a habit despite trying and trying and trying for decades. (I will never, ever floss consistently. I'm sorry, Dr. Mario. It's just not going to happen.)

For me, I find the first nine or so days of any new habit formation attempt, be it writing, exercise, or meditation, really exciting. Then it gets... boring. *Really boring.* The trick is not to stop at that point. Feels boring? Don't want to do it? Push through. Push through, until it gets automatic.

This tends to happen somewhere between that day 21 and day 40. When it gets automatic—don't you dare take a break, because after it gets automatic, it gets blissful. But that's in month three or four. Will you last that long?

I believe you will.

By the way–for a writing prompt to really do its work, *it has to surprise you*. So if you buy a writing prompt book, don't flip through it! Dammit, you probably have done so to make the decision to buy it. Ok. Fine. Flip through it very quickly. Then, forget everything you've read, and don't read ahead again. Just look at each writing prompt when you're ready to write—and not a minute sooner.

> **PROCRASTINATOR TIP:** When I started working with writing prompts, I created a new email account just for receiving writing prompts. I wanted to make sure I got my writing done before I was tempted to check email and all those other time sucks. It worked beautifully. I woke up. Made coffee. Checked *that* email account, which only had one email—my daily writing prompt. Wrote that day's scene... and only then acknowledged the existence of other email accounts and the apps on my phone.

So, to recap:

Step 1: Arrange to be fed a writing prompt every day.

Step 2: Write.

Step 3: Repeat the next day and the day after.

Write anywhere, anytime.

It's that simple.

Happy writing.

mjanecolette
July 2019

PS At the end of this guide, I tell you what you can do with your writing prompts after you've got 30, 60—or 101—days worth of them. You can flip to that chapter now... or when you're ready. I think you should just start writing, and save that chapterette for later—but please, as always when you're working with me, *please* yourself.

PS2 If you have a print copy of this guide—go ahead, deface it. Write right in the book. That way, you know you don't have to write a lot. You just have to write... a little bit. See? It's gonna be so easy.

PS3 I really love post-scripts. If you want more dirty writing secrets, they're waiting for you at:

mjanecolette.com/secrets

And if you want to stay in touch with me throughout your writing process, you can join my newsletter list, which comes with a free (fiction) e-book:

CLAIM YOUR FREE BOOK!
mjanecolette.com/loveletters

Or, write me at TellMe@mjanecolette.com.

WARNING: I write tragedy for those who like to laugh, comedy for the melancholy, and erotica for lovers who like their fantasies real. My tag line is "flirty, funny, filthy." The writing prompts that follow reflect this. They're flirty. Funny. While not really filthy (you can take them there—or not), they are intended for an adult audience.

INSTRUCTIONS: Write dirty. Write clean. Write raw.

Write.

— M. JANE COLETTE

1

She was never going to go through that again.

He was the perfect house husband, except...

3

The writing was almost indecipherable. Almost.

The floor was cold and sticky, but...

5

She hid it so well, he wasn't going to be able to find it.

Everybody knew Cupid had a sick sense of humour...

Wasn't that every woman's dream?

He tried to convince her it was because of the moon.

9

She did not want to do her Kegel exercises.

When she opened her eyes, he would not be there.

He bought a box of chocolates.

"I don't expect you to walk in them," he said.

He was going to break her heart. She knew it.

No one was surprised when the couch tipped over.

"Tell me more."

He hadn't imagined a kiss could be that bad.

It was not ideal.

It turned out he did know a thing or two about knots.

How hard could it be to seduce someone that shy?

But then, suddenly, his wings fell off.

First, she would need six pounds of cherries.

22

Maybe she was a demon after all.

The rug burn was worth it.

Sometimes, it's just about the cleavage.

"Two hearts that beat as one, my ass."

She didn't want him to know. About any of it.

It was just a bowl of fruit.

This was not the way it was supposed to end.

"What the hell do you think you're doing with that?"

No adult ever plays Twister sober.

31

There was probably a good explanation for this.

She would not be able to endure it.

33

Cinderella's glass slipper story got it all wrong.

He could be romantic, of course, but right now...

Cowboy boots.

She tried to remember that she could, indeed, fly.

He didn't get that cherry thing at all.

Orchids: a flower without shame. Just like her.

He thought she'd forgive him.

It turned out she just wasn't that flexible.

"Why do I have to bring the rope?"

She'd said it before: threesomes were always better in theory.

Revenge sex?

"That's the game we're playing. I want the key. You..."

"But why are you wearing a mask?"

"We all have our kinks. But this is not one of mine."

"I have a better use for clothespins."

She loved him as Frida loved the ugly Diego.

She would not leave empty-handed.

"Everybody fantasizes about that," he said.

Suddenly, everything made sense.

"Predator or prey?"

53

It was a deceptively domestic moment.

"You see, I prefer to be alone."

Red was not her favourite colour.

It was a perfect handful.

It wasn't temptation. It was an invitation.

Maybe it was better not to know.

59

There was just no way to make this sexy.

It didn't have to be just about the abs. Still, there they were.

He quit smoking a decade ago but man, he needed a cigarette now.

It was like the balcony scene from Romeo and Juliet, as directed by Tim Burton.

She was not going to surrender without a fight.

That was when he noticed the heavy duty anchors in the ceiling.

She stole his cab.

"Why did you have to do that?"

He didn't believe in curses, but...

The bedroom was empty, but the closet wasn't.

She insisted on the blindfold.

Eyes closed. Mouth open. And then...

"My apology for breaking the rules. There was no other way."

"And that's why we need a safe word."

He reached for the lipstick with a grin.

The scent was overpowering and she wanted to scream.

"I can't forgive that."

She long thought sunrises were over-rated.

"Hard."

She stomped on the hat. Twice. But she did not cry.

A kiss. It was just a kiss.

The towel was soaked and so was she.

He would not touch her.

Jane Austen, on acid.

"No," he said, and turned away.

Teeth. Nipple. Tongue. Then, teeth again.

"I will never bring you flowers."

Earlobes were made for this.

The batteries were dead.

"Candles? On the kitchen floor. Don't ask."

A garter belt? Really?

They would not dance.

91

"And now, you will polish my shoes."

The slap was swift.

93

Merciless. She would be merciless.

"All I can think about is thighs."

That was not the way to her heart, but...

96

A piercing?

Fortunately, torn stockings could be repurposed.

"Well, we might be able to fix the bed. But there's no saving the sheets."

Biting.

Never in a corset.

**Today's writing prompt is the last sentence you wrote yesterday.
Go.**

EPILOGUE

Next Steps

Congratulations! You've got a nice thick notebook or computer file of writing prompt pieces. What next?

There don't have to be any next steps. You don't have to do anything with the pieces you write in response to writing prompts, except to write them. Every other artist—dancer, painter, sculptor, musician—practices for the sake of practice, to main their craft muscles, and to get better. Writers are not special snowflakes: we need to practice (in private) before we create (for public consumption).

As a culture, we overvalue the product of the creative process, and we undervalue the process that makes it possible. At its core, *a writing prompt practice is about process, not product.* Write. Repeat. That's enough.

If you're over-attached to product and want to challenge yourself, try this mind-blowing exercise:

- Get your writing prompt.
- Write for five minutes.

- Delete/destroy.
- Repeat five times.
- Don't cheat. Destroy every draft.

But. If you are using writing prompts to work through the first draft of a novel—or to find or refine your concept for some bigger piece of work that's meant to see the light of publication—somewhere between the 30 and 60 day mark, you will start to think, "I think there's a novel here, I think I'm done with this part of the process." That's the time to hit pause, re-read what you've written, and start assembling it into a whole.

At this point, you probably want to stop creating new material that's going to be part of this bigger whole. Should you hit pause on your writing prompt practice? You might need to. Refining a WIP, crafting a coherent first draft from 60 separately created scenes can be an undertaking that requires all of your creative attention. Me, I maintain my writing practice in the mornings even when I'm revising. I just shift gears. So—for 60 days, every writing prompt I receive goes into creating a scene for my novel *Consequences*. Then, I'm done writing the first draft. I move on to arranging the novel, looking for holes, refining scenes. But I still start every morning with a writing practice exercise—now, I'm consciously creating stand-alone erotica shorts.

Until I'm ready to start working on the next big project, and then, I start pulling Tarot cards until I have 78 scenes of *All In The Cards* written. And then I pause. What will you do?

Whatever works for you.

If you haven't been working towards a novel, you might

notice that all, or most, of your writing prompts are kind of funky, flirty shorts. Can you turn them into a collection of erotica? Take a few of them and expand them into short stories? Do it.

The only rule here is to write.

After... the possibilities are endless.

But first—you have to write. And you did. Way to go, awesome you.

mjanecolette

ABOUT THE AUTHOR

M. Jane Colette writes tragedy for those who like to laugh, comedy for the melancholy, and erotica for lovers who like their fantasies real. She believes rules and hearts were made to be broken—ditto the constraints of genres. Her novels include *Tell Me, Consequences* (*of defensive adultery*), the award-winning rom-com *Cherry Pie Cure*, and *Text Me, Cupid*, a (slightly dirty) love story for 21st century adults who don't believe in love... but want it anyway.

Want more dirty writing secrets? They're waiting for you at

mjanecolette.com/secrets

To get a taste of M. Jane Colette's fiction via your **FREE** copy of *Taste Me: The Thinking Woman's Erotica*—a gift available exclusively to M. Jane Colette's newsletter subscribers—ask her to send you love letters:

CLAIM YOUR FREE BOOK!
mjanecolette.com/loveletters
@mjanecolette

PRAISE FOR M. JANE COLETTE

"M. Jane Colette KNOWS how to write characters. The motivations, the actions following the motives, and the reactions to the actions of the whole cast of characters (1) were so distinct from one another and (2) made PERFECT sense based on the development I as a reader saw for each character. This isn't a 2-dimensional character erotic novel. These people feel real, you will feel like you could step right into their world. You can't help but root for them."

CAUGHT BETWEEN THE PAGES,
GoodReads (on *Consequences*)

"I highly recommend it to anyone who wants a sexy, intelligent, complicated, and fascinating read about relationships that are as complex and difficult and wonderful and confusing as most relationships usually are."

GREY MATTER (on *Consequences*)

"No one does angst, family drama, hilarity, joy and eroticism better than M. Jane Colette!"

DIANA SOBOLEWSKI,
author of The Desire & Luxury Wine Series,
(on *Messy Christmas*)

"...one of those rare gems of erotic writing that offers insight and honesty into the heart and soul of a wife, mother, lover on the verge of her own world coming slowly apart."

AGARCIA8525 BOOK BLOG (on *Tell Me*)

"This book is a cure for divorce, depression, loneliness, boredom, you name it. Laugh-out-loud funny from the first page!"

HOLLY OWEN, ARWA (on *Cherry Pie Cure*)

"These characters... are not paper dolls—one always has the feeling, when reading, of having stumbled on a secret, of being let in to spy on something real."

ALYSIA CONSTANTINE,
author of *Sweet* and *Olympia Knife* (on *Consequences*)

"Warning: You may breakout in spontaneous laughter, develop cravings for baked goods and become a life-long devotee of the author!"

CARRIE AUSTIN REVIEWS (on *Cherry Pie Cure*)

I couldn't stop reading this! The waiting, the need, the want, the desire... the story is a rollercoaster and I love it.

ALYSSA LINN PALMER, author of *Midnight at the Orpheus* (on *Text Me, Cupid*)

Read more at mjanecolette.com/REVIEWS

www.ingramcontent.com/pod-product-compliance
Lightning Source LLC
Chambersburg PA
CBHW020541080526
44583CB00013B/929